THE LIVING GOSPEL

Daily Devotions for Lent 2017

Tom Fox

AVE MARIA PRESS AVE Notre Dame, Indiana

Founded in 1865, Ave Maria Press is a ministry of the United States Province of Holy Cross.

www.avemariapress.com

Paperback: ISBN-13 978-1-59471-705-5

E-book: ISBN-13 978-1-59471-706-2

Cover image "At the Foot of the Cross" © 2012 by Jeni Butler, artworkbyjeni.wix.com.

Cover and text design by John Carson.

Printed and bound in the United States of America.

Introduction

Servant of God Catherine Doherty was the founder of a mostly lay community called Madonna House. Catherine said that Lent is a time for "spring cleaning your heart." Think of this season as preparing a room for an encounter with the Lord. I love the images and challenges found in Catherine's writings. "Come Lent, make a genuflection, not so much of your knees but of your soul." You can read more of her wisdom and refreshing ideas from the book *Grace in Every Season: Through the Year with Catherine Doherty*.

Many of us have probably grown tired of the annual Lenten encouragement from parish bulletins and pulpits to give up chocolate, a favorite television show, being short tempered, or any number of other things we enjoy having or doing. The desert of Lent is an opportunity to become stronger in our faith, and fasting can help us do that. In my ministry as a deacon, I try to encourage open minds and hearts to view Lent as an opportunity to try new things along with fasting from familiar things.

Perhaps starting a fresh encounter with the gospels during Lent might be something new, maybe even sacrificial for you if you have a hard time being still long enough to read deeply. Perhaps a new effort from you might be getting up twenty minutes earlier than you normally do, and spending the extra time praying the devotions of this book. It will bring a fresh spark to your spiritual life, creating space in what I suspect is an already full life for quiet encounter with Jesus in the Lenten desert.

While I admit that I don't relish the idea of giving up things to put in my mouth, I've tried to get beyond the giving-up-chocolate view of Lent. For me, giving up coffee a few days a week is a real penance. But I also want to add practices, not just avoid things I love or enjoy. Whatever the Spirit quietly suggests to you, wouldn't it be wonderful to end this year's Lenten journey by recognizing we've been in a new desert that has brought rich connection with Christ and at least tiny sprouts of spiritual growth? Wouldn't it be nice not to have been fixated on dessert for most of Lent?

If I could express a prayerful wish for everyone who reads and uses this book of daily Lenten devotions, it would be that on the far side of the desert, just as we are about ready to leave it, Jesus is waiting for us. He asks us to join him in his Passion and Death and to rejoice with him in the magnificent glory of the Resurrection.

Well done, good and faithful servant. Well done.

Even now, says the LORD,
return to me with your whole heart,
with fasting, weeping, and mourning.
Rend your hearts, not your garments,
and return to the LORD, your God,
For he is gracious and merciful,
slow to anger, abounding in steadfast love,
and relenting in punishment.

~Joel 2:12–13

MARCH 1

ASH WEDNESDAY

BEGIN

> *Enter into silence and return to the Lord with your whole heart!*

PRAY

> A clean heart create for me, O God,
> and a steadfast spirit renew within me.
>
> *~Psalm 51:12*

LISTEN

> *Read Matthew 6:1–6; 16–18*

> "And your Father who sees in secret will repay you."
>
> *~Matthew 6:4*

Giving Up What We Give Up

A faithful elder spoke to me at the beginning of Lent a few years ago. "Deacon, you've preached about doing something new. I've been doing the same Lenten practices forever; I don't see any need to change." I'd bet there are many who seek the familiarity of (the almost comfortable) Lenten things to do. And you? Will you seek quick adoption of the things you've done in years past or try something new? Today's gospel gives us Lenten guidance: almsgiving, prayer, and fasting—in *that* order.

Other than writing a check, what sort of almsgiving would be a struggle for you this Lent? Trading personal time for something less comfortable to do?

Perhaps you can give up thirty minutes of television watching and dedicate that time to the Lenten prayer we are called to do?

Carving out time to pray and reflect with this booklet is an excellent place to begin. Praying at meal times if you don't already do so is another great habit to build. Try praying the Liturgy of the Hours or explore lectio divina. You can learn much about these with a simple Internet search. Or perhaps you prefer something more spontaneous such as writing a letter to God each morning or maybe one at day's end to help you reflect on how closely you walked with Jesus that day.

Many years ago, I heard a speaker say these words, "Lord, free me of the bondage of self." That's a good prayer. How might you "fast" from yourself? No one size fits all. What habit or routine can you surrender so as to accompany the Lord into the desert.

ACT

As I begin this Lenten journey, today I will seek to relinquish what is comfortable and journey into the desert. I will choose one new Lenten practice to undertake this year.

PRAY

Lord, hear my prayer. Let me experience a bit of welcome discomfort each day of Lent. Amen.

March 2

Thursday after Ash Wednesday

BEGIN

Enter into silence and return to the Lord with your whole heart!

PRAY

A clean heart create for me, O God,
and a steadfast spirit renew within me.

~Psalm 51:12

LISTEN

Read Luke 9:22–25

"If anyone wishes to come after me, he must deny himself and take up his cross daily and follow me."

~Luke 9:23

From Life to Life

Mother Angelica, founder of the Eternal Word Television Network, passed away last Easter. Angelica would be among those with a heavy cross experience. Yet, she carried her cross with great faith, once saying, "If you've got a cross, carry it. It's to make you holy" (*National Catholic Register*, April 17, 2016).

Jesus says if we *wish* to come after him, we need to take up our cross and follow him. Too often we catch ourselves thinking along these lines, "Well Jesus, I do wish to come after you, but I'd rather not pick up the cross of cancer; or a parent losing mental faculties; or a teen who walks away from the faith. No. I'd rather not, thank you."

It's one thing to reluctantly accept the crosses we are given. But this, fellow travelers, is what this journey is all about. The Cross is and was folly. Jesus accepted the agony and the great scandal of being hung naked, a piece of meat on a tree. All for the greater will and plan of God.

Let us journey together in imitation of Christ. Consider the joy of lives changed starting on that first Easter morning. If those around us see us joyfully, willingly, and in great faith, hope, and love accepting the crosses we've been given, our witness can be a factor in their choosing eternal life as well.

ACT

Today I will pray in gratitude for a cross I've been given. I will seek to understand how this cross might help me grow spiritually.

PRAY

I will pray to you, LORD,
    at a favorable time.
God, in your abundant kindness,
    answer me with your sure deliverance.

~Psalm 69:14

MARCH 3

FRIDAY AFTER ASH WEDNESDAY

BEGIN

Enter into silence and return to the Lord with your whole heart!

PRAY

A clean heart create for me, O God,
and a steadfast spirit renew within me.

~Psalm 51:12

LISTEN

Read Matthew 9:14–15

"Why do we and the Pharisees (disciples of John the Baptist) fast much . . . but your disciples do not fast?"

~Matthew 9:14

Fasting from Coffee or Television

I'd like to share that my wife and I give up coffee on Fridays. We've both agreed that we don't like Fridays. And we are always happy when Saturday morning comes. Is that what is supposed to happen when we fast?

Let's think about television. Fr. Francis Martin often suggests throwing out the television—completely. There's always some nervous laughter that ripples through his audiences with that remark. Many of us have little for downtime other than television; it can be switched on and not really paid attention to, but still help us unwind our minds after a long day.

So being encouraged to just throw it out is a big deal. Could we do that? Just for Lent?

Can we see any real benefit to depriving ourselves of something we enjoy, something that seems to truly add to the betterment of our lives? It isn't much of a stretch to see that fasting toughens us. In the sense of resisting the tempter in our deserts, can we become more like Christ? Stronger; more pure? Who couldn't stand a bit more purity?

Fasting also gives us wisdom. We are helped to be more prudent as we fast. How does this happen? As we fast and grow stronger in faith we begin to better understand the everyday circumstances of our lives. We perhaps think more carefully about the choices we face each day, grow more aware of others' needs, and experience gratitude more often. Most important, is that fasting helps us recall more consistently that we walk alongside Christ in all we do.

In his *Summa Theologica*, Question 147, Article 1, St. Thomas Aquinas says that fasting cleanses the soul, raises the mind, subjects one's flesh to the spirit, renders the heart contrite and humble, scatters the clouds of desire, quenches the fire of lust, and kindles the true light of chastity.

ACT

Today I will fast from one thing that is truly difficult to give up. This I will do in addition to my Lent-long fasting discipline.

PRAY

Lord, embrace my desire to draw closer to you and help me to dig deeper into the spiritual discipline of fasting. Amen.

MARCH 4

SATURDAY AFTER ASH WEDNESDAY

BEGIN

Enter into silence and return to the Lord with your whole heart!

PRAY

A clean heart create for me, O God,
and a steadfast spirit renew within me.

~Psalm 51:12

LISTEN

Read Luke 5:27–32

"I have not come to call the righteous to repentance but sinners."

~Luke 5:32

I'm All Right. I'm All Right.

I recall a scene in the classic movie *It's a Wonderful Life* where Uncle Billy comes out from a party inebriated and asks for directions home. Taking just a few steps, he falls flat on his backside. He bounces back up and says, "I'm all right. . . . I'm all right." Then off he lurches into the evening.

I think many Christians are like Uncle Billy, perhaps even some of us. We think to ourselves, "I don't murder. I haven't beaten anyone or extorted money. Basically, no problems here. No confession needed. Well, maybe I'll go once a year. I'm all right, yeah, I'm all right." Yet scripture tells us that even a good person sins seven times a day.

Lent is a perfect time to pray for clarity of heart and mind so that we can see the reality of sin in our lives. Examine your life each day. Start by simply reviewing each interaction you have with another person. Did you really notice them, listen to them, greet them kindly? Did you consider what you might do to make their day or at least that moment of interaction better for them and then do that? In short, did you bear the presence of Christ to each person you met today? If not, how will you do better tomorrow?

ACT

Today, I will find out when the sacrament of Reconciliation is available at my parish. I will schedule a time to go to confession or to attend a communal Penance/Reconciliation service this Lent.

PRAY

Lord Jesus, it isn't guilt I feel. No, it's sorrow as I realize how often and in how many ways I've not lived up to your hopes and desires for me. Heal me. Strengthen me. Forgive me. Amen.

Sunday, March 5
First Week of Lent

BEGIN

Enter into silence and return to the Lord with your whole heart!

PRAY

Give me back the joy of your salvation,
And a willing spirit sustain in me.

~Psalm 51:14

LISTEN

Read Matthew 4:1–11

At this, Jesus said to him, "Get away, Satan!"

~Matthew 4:10

Did God Really Tell You?

This story of Jesus being tempted by Satan in the desert is well known to many. But why does Jesus go into a desert for forty days? In the scriptures, the number forty often alludes to some kind of preparation. So for Jesus his forty days in the wilderness of the desert was about him being "toughened up" for his life-giving (and life-ending) ministry. As it was for Jesus, for all of us the journey toward deeper relationship with God will inevitably involve Satan.

In Genesis the first words spoken by the serpent are, "Did God really tell you not to eat from any of the trees in the garden?" The serpent is cunning and tempts Eve to set aside what God has commanded. The devil tempts Jesus with similarly cunning words, urging him to command stones to become bread to ease what must have been burning hunger. Jesus pushes back, insisting he has faith, saying in essence, "My Father will take care of my hunger. I don't need to do tricks for you to prove who I am."

Doubt. Cunning. Deceit. These are the tools of our common enemy. If you doubt the reality of the devil, he has cunningly won his first and probably most important victory in his battle to win your soul. The Church wants us to comprehend the reality of pure evil, which even the Son of Man experienced. Accepting—really accepting—the existence of both heaven and hell will serve well our Lenten journey toward submission to God's will.

ACT

Today I will sit quietly and contemplate heaven and hell and the temptations of evil in my life. If I'm uncertain of what the Church teaches, I will schedule time to do a bit of research or schedule a conversation with my pastor or another parish professional. I will pray for guidance in my quest for understanding.

PRAY

Lord God, send St. Michael the Archangel to be my protection against the wickedness and snares of evil. Teach me to turn away from sin and resist temptation to grow complacent in my spiritual growth. Amen.

Monday, March 6
First Week of Lent

BEGIN

Enter into silence and return to the Lord with your whole heart!

PRAY

Give me back the joy of your salvation,
And a willing spirit sustain in me.

~Psalm 51:14

LISTEN

Read Matthew 25:31–46

He will place the sheep on his right and the goats on his left.

~Matthew 25:33

Humbly Join the Flock

Sheep and goats were fundamental to economies of the ancient Jewish people. Both small animals provide wool, hair, or pelts, as well as milk and meat. It would seem that both would be important. So why did Jesus separate them in this parable? Those hearing Jesus would likely have readily grasped his purpose.

Sheep are gentle, docile, content to graze. They are generally most comfortable in the setting of the flock. Sheep tend to follow the shepherd, and they will avoid contact with strangers. Goats, on the other hand, are more comfortable with interaction. They are inquisitive, even nosey, getting into and eating things they ought not.

Knowing even this much about sheep and goats helps us reflect on today's gospel reading. Jesus referred to himself as the Good Shepherd. He said he knows his sheep and they know him. And so we know how Jesus hopes for us to live our lives. Whether kings or queens, presidents or heads of parliament, or poor farmers or struggling merchants, attend Mass, humbly enter daily prayer, and remain a strongly rooted member of the believing flock. The flock is family and in our acceptance that we are members of this one flock, we will have accepted that the hungry, the spiritually or physically naked, the migrant or stranger, are all part of Christ's flock as well. Even the addict or prisoner who has made repetitive mistakes, they are of his flock. Consider today how you can better serve the other members of the flock.

ACT

Today I will respond to one expressed need of my parish flock. I will check our bulletin or website to identify one new way I can give of time, talent, or treasure to my community.

PRAY

Lord Jesus, as a shepherd his sheep, so you lead me, feed me, and guard me from harm. Help me turn to you and the other members of my faith community for support and spiritual guidance. Amen.

Tuesday, March 7
First Week of Lent

BEGIN

Enter into silence and return to the Lord with your whole heart!

PRAY

Give me back the joy of your salvation,
And a willing spirit sustain in me.

~Psalm 51:14

LISTEN

Read Matthew 6:7–15

This is how you are to pray.

~Matthew 6:9

The Jesus School of Prayer

What was it that caused his disciples to ask Jesus how to pray? Was he completely entranced when he prayed? Did Jesus move his head from side to side or up and down? Did he seem joyful and at peace in his prayer? I wonder what the disciples *saw* in Jesus, in his demeanor, his attitude, his composure, that drew them to him.

Jesus taught his disciples and so us to approach prayer in a simple, straightforward manner, to call God "Father," and to trust that the Father already knows what we need. The intimacy of the Lord's Prayer that we heard about in today's gospel reading is the standard-bearer of all Christian prayer. Earthly parents usually know the needs and desires and heartaches of their children, yet it is important that children trust enough to speak those needs and desires and heart-aches to their parents. This is how love grows and children mature. So too with us as we pray. Laying our hearts bare before the Father helps us mature into fully committed disciples.

Praying as Jesus taught us, praying the Lord's Prayer, reminds us of who we are before the Father. We are people who praise God, bow to his will, humbly seek his constant care, pray to both receive and offer others forgiveness, and beg deliverance from evil. Trust today that the words Jesus prayed will bring you ever nearer to our heavenly Father.

ACT

Today I will pray for the courage to forgive someone who has hurt me or one whom I love. I realize it may take some time, but I will keep praying for the free-dom forgiveness brings.

PRAY

Heavenly Father, help me to pray as Jesus prayed. Help me to keep it basic, simple, and straightforward. Help my prayer come from my heart. Amen.

WEDNESDAY, MARCH 8
FIRST WEEK OF LENT

BEGIN

Enter into silence and return to the Lord with your whole heart!

PRAY

Give me back the joy of your salvation,
And a willing spirit sustain in me.

~Psalm 51:14

LISTEN

Read Luke 11:29–32

"There is something greater than Jonah here."

~Luke 11:32

Becoming a 2017 Prophet

How is it that so many prophets suffered rejection in their times? Even more, how could rejection happen to Jesus—the Son of God? The answer lies in the failing of humanity that often doesn't recognize a prophet. It happened with Isaiah. It happened with Jesus, leading to his eventual torture and execution.

Pope St. John Paul II said, "Freedom consists not in doing what we like, but in having the freedom to do what we ought to do." How hard this can be in a world as complex and mired in sin as ours! Most of us don't feel that we can really do much to solve the horrendous killing of infants in the womb, the wars which seem to continuously rage on, the persecution of Christians and other people of faith around the world, the neglect of the elderly, and the slaughter of innocents caught in the abomination of terrorism.

Yet, because we are Christians, we can and ought to make respect for human life at every stage and in every place a part of our regular prayer regimen and a focus of our civic action. We should be outspoken in our defense of life. In our letters, in our voting, in our social media networking, in conversations around the water cooler—wherever we are connected, we should be easily recognized as defenders of life. And, others should know us by our love.

This said, you will likely find that you become like the prophets of old, and the prophets of our times: easily ignored, pigeonholed, scoffed at.

Good! You are in the company of your brother, Jesus.

ACT

Today I will read the book of Jonah in the Bible and contemplate how I can be more courageous in defending human life.

PRAY

Lord God, help me to honor the guidance of the prophets of our times. Help me to become a Lenten prophet of repentance and conversion. Amen.

Thursday, March 9
First Week of Lent

BEGIN

Enter into silence and return to the Lord with your whole heart!

PRAY

Give me back the joy of your salvation,
And a willing spirit sustain in me.

~Psalm 51:14

LISTEN

Read Matthew 7:7–12

Ask and it will be given to you; seek and you will find; knock and the door will be opened to you.

~Matthew 7:7

And the Door Will Be Opened

Both readings at Mass today speak of petition to God for our needs. In the first reading, Esther lays prostrate on the ground and pleads with the Lord for deliverance from her enemies. The image of God opening the door at which we knock in our gospel reading from Matthew implies an eagerness on God's part to be directly involved in our lives. It suggests a personal encounter, although not necessarily the way we might have envisioned it.

Years ago, my younger brother was diagnosed with cancer. It was aggressive and already spreading into various organs of his body. At that time, I was a marginal Catholic attending church only when I felt like it. I had a foot in two worlds, like the Prodigal Son at his lower ebb.

Lukewarm, I felt uncomfortable expressing prayer and hope for my brother. Wondering what to do, I decided to attend Mass and light a candle. I don't believe I was truly inviting Jesus into my home or life. I just wanted him to fix Eddie's cancer. What happened was that the Mass really touched my heart and soul—and although I didn't recognize it, Jesus was beckoning me out of the slop pit with the swine. Not long after, I found out that my brother had had a sort of faith conversion, prior to his cancer diagnosis.

Now, more than twenty years later, I'm a deacon—in love with Jesus, his Church, and the Eucharist. It didn't happen as I would have written the story. Much happened along the way, many twists and turns, hills and valleys. Many things could not have been predicted. But this I know: This amazing journey of faith all started when I knocked and Jesus opened the door. What door along your faith journey are you ready to knock at today?

ACT

Today I will bring to prayer one petition that I carry deep in my heart. I will steady myself to accept whatever response comes from my knocking, trusting the door will be open, trying to be ready for unexpected graces.

PRAY

Gracious God, in this season of Lent, soften my heart. Help me to move closer to the door where you knock and help me be bold enough to open it. Amen.

Friday, March 10
First Week of Lent

BEGIN

Enter into silence and return to the Lord with your whole heart!

PRAY

Give me back the joy of your salvation,
And a willing spirit sustain in me.

~Psalm 51:14

LISTEN

Read Matthew 5:20–26

"Amen, I say to you, you will not be released until you have paid the last penny."

~Matthew 5:26

Bless Me Neighbor for I Have Sinned

I've met a couple people in my life who, once insulted, have refused to have meaningful conversations or any real interaction with the offending party. They simply decide *not* to relate to the other with any expectation or even hope of mending the hurt.

Have you ever experienced this with a family member or friend? Have you ever responded like this when you've been hurt? I've experienced such situations involving family members at weddings and funerals. Recently, we had a situation where a widow wouldn't turn over the cremains to other family members for a Catholic funeral.

Whether you are the one suffering rejection or the one issuing it, today's warning from the gospel tells us that there is no entry into eternal joy until the "last penny is paid." If we think we are going to enter the perfection of heaven having died with un-forgiveness or unwillingness to try to repair damage, well, it's just not going to happen.

This Lent, take time and be willing to sacrifice in order to bring healing. Summon the humility to apologize. You may not be apologizing because you agree the other person is right. Apologize because the incident happened and someone was hurt.

May I paraphrase scripture? It is crucial for husbands and wives, brothers or sisters, to go first and be reconciled, before approaching the Lord.

ACT

Today I will pray for one person whom I have offended or hurt and I will decide one small step I can take toward reconciliation.

PRAY

Our Father, forgive me my trespasses as you have forgiven me. Amen.

Saturday, March 11
First Week of Lent

BEGIN

Enter into silence and return to the Lord with your whole heart!

PRAY

Give me back the joy of your salvation,
And a willing spirit sustain in me.

~Psalm 51:14

LISTEN

Read Matthew 5:43–48

"But I say to you, love your enemies, and pray for those who persecute you."

~Matthew 5:44

The Dead Sea Scrolls and My Wife

It was early in the year 1947 when Bedouin shepherds discovered the first of what would come to be known as the Dead Sea Scrolls at Qumran in the West Bank. One of the first scrolls studied revealed the message that hatred of those who do evil was what God dictated.

We've all heard the "eye for an eye" form of response before and during the time of Jesus. But then along came the radical idea of this new teacher: love your enemies, which nearly everyone who heard him would have recognized as a message against the Law of Moses. But Jesus taught that the Father gives the gifts of sun and rain and good things to both the good and those who do evil. In essence, he taught that the Father loves the unlovable.

Earlier in her working life, my dear wife Dee started a new job in San Francisco. She entered an office and within a few days discovered a woman working nearby whom everyone else seemed to shun. They didn't want anything to do with this coworker. That very first week, Dee decided that she wasn't going to be held captive by the attitude and snarky behavior of the others. She treated that woman with friendliness and respect. They never became personal best friends, but that woman reacted with respect and courtesy and friendly behavior toward Dee. Love begets love.

God gives us a lifetime to work on these challenges that surround treating all people as beloved children of God, just as we ourselves are. As this first week of Lent comes to its end, focus your kindness on someone who needs a little neighborly love.

ACT

Today I will take time to interact with each person I encounter as a child of God, worthy of deepest respect.

PRAY

Lord, make me an instrument of your peace. Where this is hatred and discord, let me sow love and respect. Remind me each day of my journey that you wish to create a clean heart in me . . . and that a clean heart has room only for love. Amen.

SUNDAY, MARCH 12
SECOND WEEK OF LENT

BEGIN

Enter into silence and return to the Lord with your whole heart!

PRAY

Our soul waits for the Lord,
who is our help and our shield.

~Psalm 33:20

LISTEN

Read Matthew 17:1–9

"Lord, it is good that we are here."

~Matthew 17:4

Best Vacation Ever

If I asked you to name a best-ever family vacation, what would yours be? For us, it would be a summer houseboat vacation on a sprawling, crystal-clear lake in the Ozarks. Early in the summer, we were the first vacationers. There were miles of shoreline and coves to explore. We stopped the motor and jumped off the boat to swim or float on inner tubes. Our teen girls washed their hair in that clear water. That trip is still fondly talked of years later. Each of us might have said: "Lord, it is good to be here." Have you had any beautiful spiritual moments where from deep inside you would come Transfiguration words? I hope so!

I've been blessed to attend an annual clergy conference and retreat at Franciscan University in Steubenville, Ohio, for the last ten years. I have come to deeply appreciate the entire week of powerful talks, great liturgies, adoration, and other prayer times. The absolute highlight "transfiguration moment" while I'm there is to celebrate Mass with fellow priests and deacons. There I believe I witness what is happening eternally in heaven. Someone made a comment that if we could see the heavenly court surrounding us during the Eucharistic Prayer while we celebrate Mass, we just might die of happiness.

Lord, it is good that we are here. Let me return again and again.

ACT

Today, I will write about, draw a picture, or simply contemplate a time in my life that I recall as truly a moment of great brightness, of profound encounter with God. I will try to distill into a sentence or two or an image just what I experienced in that moment.

PRAY

Lord, transfigure me. Lift me from the sameness of my faith walk with you. Set my soul and my heart aflame with your love. Come Spirit of God. Let me see the unimagined love waiting for me in eternity. Amen.

Monday, March 13
Second Week of Lent

BEGIN

Enter into silence and return to the Lord with your whole heart!

PRAY

Our soul waits for the Lord,
who is our help and our shield.

~Psalm 33:20

LISTEN

Read Luke 6:36–38

Give and gifts will be given to you;
a good measure, packed together, shaken down,
and overflowing,
will be poured into your lap.

~Luke 6:37

Seats on the Fifty Yard Line

Proverbs 28:20 tells us that a "faithful man will abound with blessings." Do you ever meditate upon what the blessings of a heavenly eternity could be like? I remember a priest in his eighties who was preaching perhaps one of his last homilies. It was about God's loving generosity to those who join him in eternity. The elderly priest said, "I think it will be like we are at a football game. Our perfect joy will have us feel that we are happily rooting for both teams. We'll have seats on the fifty yard line—down low and favored with great visibility. No one in heaven will be in the 'nose-bleed' section."

"Or," he continued, "we will walk in the evening with Jesus and his Mother. We will have close and personal access to Christ. And only when we want to step elsewhere will we go off to walk with a favorite saint. We can meet our great, great-grandparents and discuss their lives. Our resurrected bodies will be like those of thirty-year-olds, with no hint of deformity. We will be perfect in our praise and gratitude to God."

What have we done to deserve these kinds of gifts? Nothing. These are the rewards for sharing with others God's infinite mercy and setting aside our judgmental ways. The gifts and joy my elderly friend preached about are the overflowing gifts of God for those of us who heed the call in today's gospel reading to "be merciful, just as your Father is merciful."

ACT

Today I will prepare for the next time I encounter someone on a city sidewalk or at a street corner asking for money. I might choose to prepare small care kits in Ziploc bags or have ready a few dollars to give. Or I can keep a prayer log and add this person to my list. I will determine not to judge, but to extend mercy in a way that seems most appropriate.

PRAY

Lord Jesus, fill me this Lent with your tender mercy and share with me the gift of unbiased love for all God's children. Amen.

TUESDAY, MARCH 14
SECOND WEEK OF LENT

BEGIN

Enter into silence and return to the Lord with your whole heart!

PRAY

Our soul waits for the Lord,
who is our help and our shield.

~Psalm 33:20

LISTEN

Read Matthew 23:1–12

Whoever exalts himself will be humbled; but whoever humbles himself will be exalted.

~Matthew 23:12

Grateful for a Priest

More than two decades ago, I began my return to a strong Catholic faith. At that time, my family and I lived in Ocala, Florida. While I recognize that the grace and the circumstances were from God, an important human part of my journey back to the Church was an Irish priest named Fr. Patrick J. O'Doherty.

In my bones, I believe Fr. Pat was a true man of God. He was not perfect, not without some irascibility. But Fr. Pat lived what he preached in the ways that witness can be given to his flock. To me and others, he was both mentor and witness.

On the important issue of witness, each week Fr. Pat visited hospitals and nursing homes. He went to jails and prisons. I took Fr. Pat for a Florida prison visit and he was spellbinding in his outreach to the prisoners. One insight he liked to share was that the only difference between them (the prisoners) and himself was that they had been caught.

He would drop in to visit new families. If convenient for parishioners, he would come in and bless their home. He asked his parishioners to sign up at the office and invite him to dinner. He had no favorites, no significant special relationships. He had dinner with any who wanted to have him.

He received the bishop's permission to have the Blessed Sacrament in residence in his own quarters. So he was able to be more fully in the presence of Jesus even when he was off duty. The witness of this gentle, humble man changed my life and inspired me not only to return to my Catholic faith, but eventually to seek ordination as a deacon. Fr. Pat humbled himself and I suspect God has greatly exalted him.

ACT

Today I will pray in thanksgiving for priests who have faithfully served our Church. I will pray also for mercy and patience for those who struggle in their ministry.

PRAY

Oh Mary, Mother of God, I ask your renewed and continuing intercession for each of our priests: the strong, the good, the weak, and those in danger of losing their way. In Jesus' name, we pray. Amen.

WEDNESDAY, MARCH 15
SECOND WEEK OF LENT

BEGIN

Enter into silence and return to the Lord with your whole heart!

PRAY

Our soul waits for the Lord,
who is our help and our shield.

~Psalm 33:20

LISTEN

Read Matthew 20:17–28

Command that these two sons of mine sit, one at
right and the other at your left, in your kingdom.

~Matthew 20:21

Mama's Boy

Today's gospel presents the epitome of a parent for
better grades on a child's report card. Picture the scene:
Were the sons standing behind her, heads down and
afraid to look up at the Teacher? After all his miracles
and the excited, cheering crowds who followed, the
disciples must have been pretty sure they were headed
toward an unbelievable victory party of some sort.
To sit on the left and right of the king—these were
the most favored seats in biblical times. But today's
scripture reminds us that our ways are not his ways. To
follow Jesus, we must walk the rutty road to Calvary.

I've shared with you about Servant of God
Catherine Doherty. She's the founder of Madonna
House, a mostly lay organization headquartered in

Combermere, Canada. Catherine told her members there is room on the back of Jesus' Cross. He's waiting for his true followers there. That's also where victory comes from. To our human ways of thinking, this just doesn't seem sensible.

My wife and I have a friend who has a life-consuming disease that will gradually, but surely, lead to bodily immobility and an agonizing death. She has sent out cards with words of inspiration to us and to others. We pray; we are quietly very sorry for her condition. She knows about participation in the sufferings of Christ. She is willing to drink the cup and open her being to the life-changing gift of the Cross of Christ.

ACT

Today I will contemplate the Cross of Christ. I will think of the one action that gives me the most discomfort but that I believe is part of my Christian calling. I will climb the Cross, and in humility, surrender by doing that very thing.

PRAY

Dear Jesus, by your Cross and resurrection, you have set us free. Teach me your ways, so that I too may surrender to the will of the Father. Amen.

Thursday, March 16
Second Week of Lent

BEGIN

Enter into silence and return to the Lord with your whole heart!

PRAY

Our soul waits for the Lord,
who is our help and our shield.

~Psalm 33:20

LISTEN

Read Luke 16:19–31

And lying at his door was a poor man named Lazarus.

~Luke 16:20

Now You See Me

Consider the following meditation points for today. Why is the hungry man with open sores at the door of the rich man instead of down at a busy intersection? And why is the dog being fed and not Lazarus? Is there something beautiful associated with an angel carrying our soul to heaven? After death, Lazarus is in a "brightness" while the rich man is in a darkness. Yet they can see each other.

Luke spoke often of hunger and illness. He must have often seen that the rich can afford all they need but they can't truly be separated from the needy around us. Some people will do a great deal to help pet care and pet adoption facilities. Some may care for strays. Yet many of these won't first consider giving to help starving humans. I cannot understand this, but surely neglecting our fellow humans is a rejection of the mercy of God. Yes, we are called to care for all of creation, and surely there is plenty to go around, if only we find the will to do so.

Luke writes often about the idea of light. In today's gospel parable, those who achieve eternal reward are in eternal light. Those who fail suffer eternal darkness. May God's Spirit give us fresh and new points to ponder each time we return as beggars before the Wisdom throne.

ACT

Today I will engage someone in conversation whom I would ordinarily barely acknowledge. I will greet them as one made in the image and likeness of God.

PRAY

Make me worthy, Lord, to serve those people throughout the world who live and die in poverty and hunger. Let me be your hands to feed and clothe and shelter them. Amen.

Friday, March 17
Second Week of Lent

BEGIN

Enter into silence and return to the Lord with your whole heart!

PRAY

Our soul waits for the Lord,
who is our help and our shield.

~Psalm 33:20

LISTEN

Read Matthew 21:33–43, 45–46

Finally, He sent his son to them, thinking, "They will respect my son."

~Matthew 21:37

Better Than "Them"

In the first Mass reading from Genesis today, there is the story of the seventeen-year-old Joseph, so loved by his father that he is given a multicolored coat. Dyes were special and costly, and this extravagance caused jealousy in the other sons, the brothers of Joseph. They ultimately capture Joseph and sell him into slavery for twenty pieces of silver.

In today's gospel, the growing jealousy of the chief priests and Pharisees is tweaked by Jesus' parable about the landowner (God the Father). Jesus shares the challenging image of the Father who, after prophets are rejected, finally sends his favorite son. Pride and arrogant self-image blocked the truth in the leaders of the Jews. And Jesus becomes the stone rejected by the builders. Yet he became the cornerstone of the new faith and he was most pleasing in the eyes of the Father (see Matthew 21:42b).

There are so many ways that we too can struggle with the sin of pride. Driving past that poorly clad guy begging at the corner: "I'm so glad I'm not lazy, wasting my life like him." Going to daily Mass and thinking judgmentally about those who don't get to Sunday Mass. Here's another judgment: "We Catholics have the better of it all, don't you agree?"

Yes, there are so many ways we can find the molecules or pebbles of pride in us. Lent is the opportunity to invite humility to a greater place in our mind and heart.

ACT

Today I will find the Litany of Humility. I will promise to include it in my prayer time at least once a week. (Here's one online source for the Litany: http://www.catholic365.com/article/1619/why-would-anyone-pray-the-litany-of-humility.html.)

PRAY

Lord, free me from the bondage of self. Amen.

Saturday, March 18
Second Week of Lent

BEGIN

Enter into silence and return to the Lord with your whole heart!

PRAY

Our soul waits for the Lord,
who is our help and our shield.

~Psalm 33:20

LISTEN

Read Luke 15:1–3, 11–32

Then let us celebrate with a feast, because this son of mine was dead, and has come to life again; he was lost, and has been found.

~Luke 15:23b–24a

Even as You Read

Over the years, we've become accustomed to the familiar story of the Prodigal Son. We know the beginning: "Give me your money now; I don't want to wait till you are no longer in the picture." We know the middle action of the not really repentant son: "I will return to my father just so I have certainty of at least enough food to eat." We know the end: a party for the repatriated son. The older brother scowls, in failure to see and share in his father's love.

I too am a prodigal son. I returned to the Father. My return has been beautiful. I wasn't asked to work in the swine pits. I wasn't humiliated on my return.

Instead, he wrapped me in the mantle of love. When I stumble, he continues to forgive and to love.

I hope. And yes, today I am in prayer that you are deeply in love with Jesus and his Church. I hope that you have not glossed over today's gospel. Seek to come to a glowing fire of appreciation for the family (his family) that you belong to.

And may I close with a recommendation? Please buy and read (or listen to the audio version of) *The Return of the Prodigal Son* by the late Henri Nouwen. All of this book originates from Nouwen's visit to Russia to see the original Rembrandt painting. His reflections are marvelous.

ACT

Starting today, I will begin work to return to loving (or at least peaceful) relationship with anyone or any organization that has been a problem in my journey.

PRAY

Dear Heavenly Father, today I stop and pray for the wonderful evangelistic work being done by organizations that invite, coach, and disciple people to return to the Catholic Faith. They are too numerous to do justice to all of them, but Father, I ask your blessing and help for organizations such as Catholics Come Home, St. Paul Street Evangelization, and Catholic Answers. Bless also the work of Catholic radio and television throughout the world. Amen.

Sunday, March 19
Third Week of Lent

BEGIN

Enter into silence and return to the Lord with your whole heart!

PRAY

Come, let us bow down in worship
Let us kneel before the LORD who made us.

~Psalm 95:6

LISTEN

Read John 4:5–42

Many of the Samaritans of that town began to believe in Him because of the word of the woman who testified, "He told me everything I have done."

~John 4:39

A New Kind of Lenten Reconciliation

There was an elderly widow who struggled with alcohol addiction. She was a functioning alcoholic, going for weeks without a crash. But every few months, when her addiction, loneliness, and weakness became too much, she would close her miniblinds and refuse to answer her door or her phone. In that dark tomb, she would drink herself into stupor. Days later, once able to be in contact, a few elders closest to her would try to encourage her back to normal behavior, which often included daily Mass and other devotions. Most parishioners didn't know of this.

Are you familiar with the so-called gift of reading souls that several saints have had? This meant that the saints could read the soul and the conscience of visitors and those going to confession. While many saints were reported to have this capability, two well-known saints who were so gifted were Padre Pio and John Vianney.

These priests knew (in a spiritual but also a real sense) what sins and struggles one had. This could be a great help to a powerful confession. It could also be confrontational if a penitent would try to shade or ignore things which rightly ought to be confessed.

What would your Lenten reconciliation be like if you met Jesus at the well? And if he told you everything you have done? Would it change the way you expressed things to your confessor? Would you leave in those things which are uncomfortable to talk about?

ACT

I will put myself into the midday light of truth at the well in Samaria. I understand Samaria to be a way of being an outsider—a sinner. I will ask Jesus to guide me in preparation, true preparation, for an open confession of any and all sins from the first commandment to the tenth commandment.

PRAY

Lord Jesus: How many times and how many ways have I discussed my sins in the confessional in a way that tries to justify my behaviors or reactions? Help me to seek an honest meeting with your Divine Mercy. Amen.

MONDAY, MARCH 20
THIRD WEEK OF LENT

Enter into silence and return to the Lord with your whole heart!

Come, let us bow down in worship
Let us kneel before the LORD who made us.

~Psalm 95:1

Read Luke 4:24–30

When the people in the synagogue heard this, they were all filled with fury.

~Luke 4:28

We Are All One Body

Two thousand years ago, Jews were certain of their status as the Chosen People. In today's gospel, those in the synagogue were certain: they had the Torah; they had Moses' teachings. They were so certain of their views that any other ideas were grounds for execution. So too, many Catholics and indeed other Christians have been raised with the conviction of being a specially chosen people, having all the answers and somehow exclusive access to the truth about God. Sadly this sensibility is often exaggerated to the point of nearly impenetrable self-assurance. It is a great gift to be certain in one's faith, but with that tremendous blessing comes the risk of growing deaf to the prophets among us.

Today we see so many ongoing conflicts that damage, rather than refine, our political, religious, social, and economic relationships not only within our country but also between nations, and sadly within our own Church. Yet Jesus calls us to remain humble and so able to hear the clarion call of the prophets in our midst who call us constantly to conversion of heart, to keep steady to the path of discipleship that Christ laid before us.

This week of Lent, let us pray for and love our separated brothers and sisters in Christ and let us hold firmly to the faith of our Fathers. Let us give witness to the reality of the Real Presence, Christ present in our eucharistic celebrations. Let us bear prophetic witness to love and mercy, fully knowing that we, like Jesus, will be rejected by many.

ACT

Today, I will examine my life and decide on three ways to be a prophetic witness of love and mercy for those whom I encounter. I will be especially attentive to anyone whom I know is hurting.

PRAY

Eternal Father, I praise you for sending your Son to be one of us and to save us. Look upon your divided people with mercy. Help us to become one in love. Amen.

Tuesday, March 21
Third Week of Lent

BEGIN

Enter into silence and return to the Lord with your whole heart!

PRAY

Come, let us bow down in worship
Let us kneel before the LORD who made us.

~Psalm 95:1

LISTEN

Read Matthew 18:21–35

"Lord, if my brother sins against me, how often must I forgive him?"

~Matthew 18:21

But This . . . This Is Unforgivable

The totality of the gospels suggests to us how frail and even broken the apostles were, although they were chosen and taught by Jesus himself. In today's gospel, here comes Peter up to the Lord. You can tell he's frustrated. You know before he speaks that he can be brash, opinionated, and impatient. You sense that someone has done something such that Peter feels he has been wronged. His tone of voice shares this as well. We could imagine it this way:

"Jesus, you know how much Judas irritates me. I don't know why you ever asked him to join us. I've tried to get along even with him. He keeps telling me to 'shut up, shut up.' How often should I forgive him, before you give me permission to deck him?"

"Peter, dear Peter. If you want to be my follower, you must learn to forgive, truly forgive, seventy times seven times or more. These episodes which upset you, Peter, are just the failings of human frailty. And this forgiveness you grant now is good training for you so that you may have strength to forgive when what they do to you seems unforgivable."

God has *never* asked us to forget. Nor does he suggest we not seek justice. Jesus asks us to come to a point of forgiving. We've all heard heartwrenching stories of people whose lives have been shattered by horrible, deliberate acts of others, and yet find a way to forgive. Forgiveness requires a choice to choose love and mercy over hostility, anger, and ultimately our own wounded psyches and souls. Don't let anger, pain, or even horror consume you or control your life. Work at forgiving.

ACT

Today I will recall one harm done to me and pray that I may forgive and heal. And I will consider one harm I have done another and pray to be forgiven.

PRAY

Many are the sorrows of the wicked one,
  but mercy surrounds the one who trusts in the
  LORD.

~Psalm 32:10

WEDNESDAY, MARCH 22
THIRD WEEK OF LENT

BEGIN

Enter into silence and return to the Lord with your whole heart!

PRAY

Come, let us bow down in worship
Let us kneel before the LORD who made us.

~Psalm 95:1

LISTEN

Read Matthew 5:17–19

"Amen, I say to you, until heaven and earth pass away, not the smallest letter or the smallest part of a letter will pass from the law, until all things have taken place."

~Matthew 5:18

Don't Change a Hair for Me

In teaching about the Law of the Jewish people, Jesus seems to suggest (command?) that literal enforcement (keeping) of the Law to the absolute last detail is what followers would be obligated to do. But later in the Acts of the Apostles, the apostles struggled with how to be faithful. What about dietary laws? What about circumcision? Were lambs still to be slaughtered with blood splashed on the sides of altars? What should they do about the six hundred and more laws of Jewish faith practice? How to cleanse oneself in those times wasn't a matter of just washing hands. Oh no. Water had to run down the arms to keep any dirt at a higher elevation from defiling the clean hands below. From such struggles, it would seem the early believers were called to see Jesus' words in a much broader sense.

In retrospect, Jesus was giving the new spirit of the law about purification. Be clean of heart (see Matthew 5:8). Do not encourage one to seek the revenge of an "eye for an eye." Instead, "blessed are the peacemakers" (see Matthew 5:9).

We ought always to seek the guidance and current practice of the Church at large. In a general sense, after his Ascension, the followers of Jesus began to signal that keeping reverent practice in our hearts is the goal. Doing that while letting go of smaller changes which happen from time to time is acceptable.

ACT

In my Lenten visits to church, let me display a deep and inspired reverence in all of the practices that I do. Let them not be for "show," but rather because they flow from entry into and participation in liturgies in the holiest place on earth.

PRAY

The Law of the LORD is perfect,
   refreshing the soul.
The decree of the LORD is trustworthy,
   giving wisdom to the simple.

~Psalm 19:8

Thursday, March 23
Third Week of Lent

BEGIN

Enter into silence and return to the Lord with your whole heart!

PRAY

Come, let us bow down in worship
Let us kneel before the LORD who made us.

~Psalm 95:1

LISTEN

Read Luke 11:14–23

Others, to test him, asked him for a sign from heaven.

~Luke 11:16

If This Is How You Treat Your Friends . . .

I remember my late mother wanted someone to be with her when she died. She didn't want to pass alone. I have experienced or sensed this in others I have been with in serious illness or at the hour of death. It speaks of our human desire for the comfort and companionship of loved ones in times of distress.

Behind the healing of the mute person, scripture conveys that Jesus *always* meets us in illness, disease, or our approach to death. In the verses just prior to today's gospel (Luke 11:9–13) Jesus promises ("I tell you, ask and you will receive. . . .") that any prayer we offer in faith, even while in our human weakness or brokenness, is heard and will be responded to.

In the gospel today, those hardened of heart are wrapped in skepticism. They challenge the Lord: "Come on Jesus, give us a sign. Make the sun spin. Make my husband become more loving. Make my cancer disappear . . . then I'll know you're really listening. And caring."

Do we know someone who is nearing the end of life? Do we have a parent or a relative who is experiencing early dementia or other decline? Are we ourselves alternating between periods of joy followed by depression? We know Jesus didn't heal everyone from every unfortunate circumstance. Was there perhaps a greater value, an unseen aspect of God's will in these decisions?

Ask for the gift of increase in faith. This will be made manifest by two reactions: heightened acceptance and then gratitude for Jesus' presence in all of our life experiences.

ACT

Today, I will look for any circumstances that don't seem fair, appropriate, or loving. I will ask Jesus for the gift of growing faith and acceptance, and the courage to bring his healing presence to these situations.

PRAY

Lord Jesus, teach me this day to bring your tender love and undying mercy to those around me who are hurting. Give me your strength to show them your compassion and work to bring justice to their lives. Amen.

Friday, March 24
Third Week of Lent

Enter into silence and return to the Lord with your whole heart!

PRAY

Come, let us bow down in worship
Let us kneel before the LORD who made us.

~Psalm 95:1

LISTEN

Read Mark 12:28–34

"You shall love the Lord your God with all your heart, with all your soul, with all your mind, and with all your strength."

~Mark 12:30

"If I Were a Rich Man"

A favorite movie of mine is the delightful *Fiddler on the Roof*. It depicts what an authentic, simple Jewish faith and relationship with the Almighty God would look like.

The lead character is Tevya. And he understands how to involve God in everything. Walks. Prayer. Worship. Tradition. Conversation. To Tevya, God is an intimate, approachable friend. "You know Lord . . . would it really ruin some plan of yours if I were born rich, instead of poor?"

Tevya understands that the most important commandment is the first. It existed for thousands of years before. It was meant to exist forever. It was the declaration of faith in the one God said in the morning and in the evening. It was to be his deathbed confession of faith.

In the gospel, when asked what is most important, Jesus' responds with a part of the words from the Shema. This prayer, rooted in the first commandment, was and is a most important liturgical prayer for the Jewish people. They wake every morning and recall that God is the center of everything.

Let us be like Tevya and our Jewish brothers and sisters as they pray the Shema. Let us walk with God and really talk with God; let us show him that he is the center of our lives. Then we will truly be rich. "Hear O people of Lenten journey, the Lord is our God, the Lord is One."

ACT

Today I will spend time before the Blessed Sacrament or at least schedule a time in the next day or two. I will speak to Christ from my heart. I will walk in a park or along a jogging path and I will speak to the Lord from my lips.

PRAY

My travels and my rest you mark;
with all my ways you are familiar.
Even before a word is on my tongue,
LORD, you know it all.

~Psalm 139:3–4

SATURDAY, MARCH 25
THIRD WEEK OF LENT

BEGIN

Enter into silence and return to the Lord with your whole heart!

PRAY

Come, let us bow down in worship
Let us kneel before the LORD who made us.
~Psalm 95:1

LISTEN

Read Luke 18:9–14

"For everyone who exalts himself will be humbled,
and the one who humbles himself will be exalted."
~Luke 18:14

The Perfume of Humility

For perhaps fifteen or more years, I have been a fan and follower of Fr. Larry Richards. I know some think he's a bit much. And some hear his challenging, straightforward manner of speaking and wouldn't at all think of him as having humility. I disagree. About humility, Fr. Larry says, "You will never be a great saint, unless you know that you are a great sinner. A sinner has a form of subtle pride . . . the kind that gets in there and robs us of salvation . . . because it's the pride that says I want to do things my way . . . I'm darned good. I have seen it in priests. I've seen it in parish staffs and volunteers."

Fr. Larry continues: "Let me give you a hint—God doesn't need you and He doesn't need me! Sometimes we think He does! God doesn't need you or me—BUT

He has called us. And when you and I come before Him and acknowledge who I am without Him—then He can do great things for me and with me."

One of the ways that we can do this is to learn the Jesus prayer. "Lord Jesus Christ, Son of the Living God, have mercy on me, a sinner." My former pastor Fr. Pat's version was simpler: "Jesus, I love you. Possess me." He said it hundreds and hundreds of times a day. It's hard to be proud and arrogant when you sincerely pray for Jesus to take possession of you.

ACT

Today I will pray for, and work on acquiring, a greater degree of humility. Because I need it.

PRAY

O Jesus! meek and humble of heart, hear me.
From the desire of being esteemed, deliver me, Jesus.
Amen.

Sunday, March 26
Fourth Week of Lent

BEGIN

Enter into silence and return to the Lord with your whole heart!

PRAY

Even though I walk in the dark valley
I fear no evil; for you are at my side.

~Psalm 23:4a

LISTEN

Read John 9:1–41

So they said to him, "How were your eyes opened?" He replied, "The man called Jesus made clay and anointed my eyes and told me, 'Go to Siloam and wash.'
So I went there and washed and was able to see."

~John 9:10–11

Seeing from Our Heart

God's holy and inspired scripture speaks to us on so many levels. Consider the unimaginable joy of the man born blind when the first and most glorious sight that he saw was the face of the Lord Jesus. Back at the turn of this century, two song writers (Debra Evans Price and Paul Baloche) tapped into that desire found in most of our inner beings. They penned the words which have given thousands of Christian believers a different way to seek a vision of Christ. I'm speaking of the popular praise song "Open the Eyes of My Heart."

How often I have been in praise and worship settings and I have seen people with their eyes closed, a hand raised in supplication. The repeated words of the song and sometimes with tears caused by fervent petition: "I want to see you." The Spirit beckons us to repeat the refrain over and over.

Are you struggling to see Jesus in the midst of something you are experiencing? Are you in your Lenten desert all alone? St. Paul gives us encouragement: "What eye has not seen and ear has not heard, and what has not entered the human heart, what God has prepared for those who love him, this God has revealed to us through the Spirit. . . . At present, we see indistinctly as in a mirror, but then face to face." (1 Corinthians 2:9–10; 13:12).

ACT

Today I will sit quietly for ten minutes and think about something in my life that is confusing to me. If I face a complicated choice, I will pray for clear vision to make a good decision. If I am confused about a different kind of situation, I will pray for courage and wisdom to better understand my role in the matter.

PRAY

Open the eyes of my heart, Lord. Open the eyes of my heart. Amen.

Monday, March 27
Fourth Week of Lent

BEGIN

Enter into silence and return to the Lord with your whole heart!

PRAY

Even though I walk in the dark valley
I fear no evil; for you are at my side.

~Psalm 23:4a

LISTEN

Read John 4:43–54

"Unless you people see signs and wonders, you will not believe."

~John 4:48

Signs and Wonders

The Bible is full of stories of God signaling to his people of his unwavering love. Genesis tells us that God gave Noah a sign. Then, there's the story of Moses and the burning bush on Mount Horeb and that of the three men dancing in the fiery hot furnace of persecution, who remain unharmed—to name but a few.

We know that Jesus also used signs: he touched lepers as a sign of his compassion and healing. Jesus moistened dirt to make clay—reminding us of the creation of man from the dirt. There were other signs, like the multiplication of the loaves and fishes.

In our times, we receive ashes as a sign of our mortality and an ancient sign intended to show willingness to repent. The ashes that mark our foreheads on Ash Wednesday are a sign that we Catholics are willing to accept the call to Lenten prayer, fasting, and almsgiving.

Yes, Lord. But what about some *powerful* signs today? Part the waters (or the traffic or the snow) so I can get to work on time. Heal my baby's croup. Now. And Jesus replies: "Unless you people see signs and wonders, you will not believe." So, perhaps our lives are filled with signs of God's enduring presence—wonderful acts of courage, kindness, hope in the deepest darkness. Perhaps we have only to stop and notice these things. Signs of God's love are most often not dramatic or showy or earth shaking. But signs of God's love and compassion fill our world and they can bring wonderful transformation, if we but pay attention.

ACT

Today I will watch for signs of God's love and mercy in my life. I will pause and give him thanks when I see these. I will find a way to be for others a living sign of love.

PRAY

Bless the Lord, all you works of the Lord,
   praise and exalt him above all forever.

~Daniel 3:57

Tuesday, March 28
Fourth Week of Lent

BEGIN

Enter into silence and return to the Lord with your whole heart!

PRAY

Even though I walk in the dark valley
I fear no evil; for you are at my side.

~*Psalm 23:4a*

LISTEN

Read John 5:1–16

Now that day was a Sabbath.

~*John 5:9b*

Rise, and Walk

In the lands of the ancient Jewish people not only did water sustain life but it was also a sign of restored fertility. Water reminded the people of a primeval paradise whereas dryness and arid ground were signs of abandonment and even death.

But what's behind the idea of water "stirred up" and having power to restore? Jesus said the man in today's gospel that had been lying at the pool ill for thirty-eight years didn't need to get into the pool. Jesus confirms that he is the Lord of the Sabbath: "Rise, take up your mat, and walk" (John 5:8). Jesus rules the Sabbath.

The lesson for today? Scripture tells us that Jesus provides renewal, refreshment, and restoration, and it comes from the new temple on the Sabbath of the

Resurrection. Ought we to seek healing on Sundays? During the remaining days of Lent, let us seek to be renewed by the powerful waters flowing from Sunday Mass. Then, through our words and actions, may we honor and keep holy the remainder of the day.

ACT

Today as I prepare for the coming of the risen Lord, I will ask him to renew my love and zeal for the Sabbath.

PRAY

But whoever drinks the water I shall give will never thirst; the water I shall give will become in him a spring of water welling up to eternal life.

~John 4:14

WEDNESDAY, MARCH 29
FOURTH WEEK OF LENT

BEGIN

Enter into silence and return to the Lord with your whole heart!

PRAY

Even though I walk in the dark valley
I fear no evil; for you are at my side.

~Psalm 23:4a

LISTEN

Read John 5:17–30

"Do not be amazed at this, because the hour is coming in which all who are in the tombs will hear his voice and come out."

~John 5:28–29a

Which Road Am I On?

The Choices We Face is the longest running Catholic television program in the world. Each week, Ralph Martin, president of Renewal Ministries, and co-host Peter Herbeck share guests, education, inspiration, and challenge.

Martin once said, "If I were to describe how the average Catholic looks at the world today, I'd describe it like this, 'Broad and wide is the way to heaven, and almost everyone is going that way. And narrow is the door that leads to hell and hardly anyone is going that way.' But you know what, that's just the opposite of the situation that Jesus describes."

Jesus seems to be saying, "Broad and wide is the way that leads to destruction, and many are traveling that way. And narrow is the door that leads to life and few there are that are traveling that way and finding it." Now Jesus didn't tell us this is the way it has to be—people that are on the broad way don't have to stay on it. That's where we come in, where our prayer comes in. That's where our witness comes in and where our love takes hold.

Lent is the opportunity to face this eternal reality. Jesus says, "Amen, Amen, I say to you, the hour is coming. . . ." Are we doing everything possible to prepare for that day of reckoning? Do we have one foot on the narrow way and one foot on the broad way? It won't work. We have got to choose.

ACT

Today, I will decide on one thing that is not bringing life to me to get rid of. I will ask the Spirit to guide me on the narrower path to life in Christ.

PRAY

My Lord, Jesus, teach me to follow your ways, to choose justice, mercy, and love over the ways of sin and death. Help me do no harm this day. Amen.

THURSDAY, MARCH 30
FOURTH WEEK OF LENT

BEGIN

Enter into silence and return to the Lord with your whole heart!

PRAY

Even though I walk in the dark valley
I fear no evil; for you are at my side.

~Psalm 23:4a

LISTEN

Read John 5:31–47

"The works that the Father gave me to accomplish, these works that I perform testify on my behalf."

~John 5:36b

Your Life Testimony

One of the themes conveyed in today's gospel has to do with human praise and testimony. Jesus said that he didn't accept human praise, but he suggests rather directly that coming to him, seeking him, would gain his disciples the praise and the testimony of the Father.

Lent gives us the opportunity to reflect on our life's testimony, to ponder the question, to what or to whom does my life give witness? If you were to write your own epitaph, would it say, "This person was always at the work of the Father"?

There's still time and grace enough to change the direction of your life. Our Lenten fast, prayer, and almsgiving call us each to repentance, to turning back to the Lord. What is your witness this day?

ACT

Today I will contemplate how I can be a faithful witness to the Good News of Jesus Christ. How do I testify to the tender mercy of God and the saving power of Christ's Resurrection by the way I live each day?

PRAY

Lord Jesus, please send your Spirit of guidance and fortitude. Lead me to be a powerful witness to the mystery of your death and resurrection. Amen.

Friday, March 31
Fourth Week of Lent

BEGIN

Enter into silence and return to the Lord with your whole heart!

PRAY

Even though I walk in the dark valley
I fear no evil; for you are at my side.

~Psalm 23:4a

LISTEN

Read John 7:1–2, 10, 25–30

The Jewish feast of Tabernacles was near.

~John 7:2

Trust While on the Journey

Today's gospel has Jesus seeking to head toward and participate in the Feast of Tabernacles, but of necessity, being careful because he knew that momentum was building to execute him. It was close, but it was not yet his time.

There is some beautiful symmetry between the way Jesus approached Jerusalem and this time of celebration. During the Feast of Tabernacles, or *Sukkot*, Jews traveled as on pilgrimage, and gathered in Jerusalem to remember God's providential care in the wilderness and to celebrate in gratitude for the year's harvest. But there was a second reason for Tabernacles—it helped the Jewish people look forward to a time when an expected Messiah would come, and all nations (including the Gentiles) would travel to

Jerusalem to worship the Lord. Pilgrims traveled in part to pray for the messiah's arrival. And in the gospel, Jesus comes as the one to save all people. Christianity grew out of Judaism, and much of the way we worship as Catholics is derived from Jewish worship. We do well, as did the ancient Jews, to recall our total dependence upon our loving Father.

Servant of God Catherine Doherty used to teach about the faith and trust of Russian pilgrims. They would leave their homes carrying only food enough for one day. They trusted God to provide for the duration whether for days or weeks. With such noble examples, we ought never to walk in the dark valley alone, but rather realize we continue in a long line of faithful peoples on our journey toward the Father.

ACT

As I think about my life this day, I will consider an area that causes me anxiety or undue stress. I will pray for the gifts of trust and courage to find peace in that experience.

PRAY

Lord Jesus, illumine my way. Teach me patience and give me clarity of mind and a steadfast heart. Walk with me and be my guide as together we journey to the Father. Amen.

Saturday, April 1
Fourth Week of Lent

BEGIN

Enter into silence and return to the Lord with your whole heart!

PRAY

Even though I walk in the dark valley
I fear no evil; for you are at my side.

~Psalm 23:4a

LISTEN

Read John 7:40–53

So the Pharisees answered them, "Have you also been deceived?"

~John 7:43

What Would Jesus Do?

Some time ago, a special priest gave me one of those cloth bracelets with the visible letters on it: WWJD. I know it sounds out of fashion by today's standards. After some years, I pulled it out of the drawer and put it on. A couple things happened. The first was this: I became so aware of the bracelet being on and visible to others that it began to cause me to change my own behavior. I didn't want to be seen to be rude to anyone, anywhere, in any situation. The bracelet caused me to smile a lot more than I previously had smiled. I smiled at the bank, in the supermarket, walking through a park, and even while parking my car. Putting on the cloth armor of Christ led me to change my interaction with others—in short, to be more loving.

The second thing that happened had to do with perceptions of me by others. I was sure that some who would see me with my bracelet would pigeonhole me as someone who has become a fanatic—"over the top" about this religion stuff. And sure enough, it happened.

After a while, I didn't wear the bracelet anymore. I put it back in the drawer, along with whatever my thinking was at the time. I am pretty sure I said to Jesus, "Someday, I would like to be a follower." But I wasn't ready right then.

How about you? Someday, would you like to be a follower of Jesus?

ACT

Today, I will surrender to Jesus all my concern about what others think of me. I will give today to him, to guide my every word and action.

PRAY

I place my trust you, O Lord. God, I praise your promise; in you I trust, I do not fear. Amen.

SUNDAY, APRIL 2
FIFTH WEEK OF LENT

BEGIN

Enter into silence and return to the Lord with your whole heart!

PRAY

With the Lord there is mercy
And fullness of redemption.

~Psalm 130:7

LISTEN

Read John 11:1–45.

And when he said this, he cried out in a loud voice, "Lazarus, come out!" The dead man came out, tied hand and foot with burial bands, and his face was wrapped in a cloth. So Jesus said to them, "Untie him and let him go."

~John 11:43–44

Release Me, Lord

Near the beginning of Mass, we pray the Penitential Rite, sometimes using the Greek version, *"Kyrie, eleison. Christe, eleison. Kyrie, eleison."* The Greek translation is powerful beyond its literal meaning: "Release us, Lord, unbind us." We also pray this in the prayer that Jesus taught us, the "Our Father." Forgive us our sins as we forgive—or release us, as we release those who harm us. In today's gospel reading, Jesus calls Lazarus from the tomb to new life and invites his friends to unbind him and set him free.

As Jesus arrives at the tomb, burdened not only with his own grief but also with the deep sorrow of Mary, Martha, and other friends who have gathered, he is deeply moved. In his grief, Jesus first thanks God, and then he calls Lazarus forth from the tomb. And Lazarus comes to life, bound by the wrappings of the funeral cloth. And Jesus says to his friends, "Untie him and let him go." Lazarus lets himself be freed, released from his bondage. We are often bound by sin and an incapacity or even an unwillingness to forgive. Jesus waits for us in merciful love and tender compassion. He waits to set us free.

ACT

I will identify two things from which I seek release, healing, or forgiveness. Imagining that I can hold these things in my hands. I will pray to open my heart and hands and let Jesus heal me.

PRAY

Gracious God, release me from my sins and all the wounds I carry in my heart. Unbind me and set me free. Amen.

MONDAY, APRIL 3
FIFTH WEEK OF LENT

BEGIN

> *Enter into silence and return to the Lord with your whole heart!*

PRAY

> With the Lord there is mercy
> And fullness of redemption.
>
> *~Psalm 130:7*

LISTEN

> *Read John 8:1–11*

> "Let the one among you who is without sin be the first to throw a stone."
>
> *~John 8:7*

Judging Sin and Not People

How many of us really believe that fornication and adultery are seriously sinful? We might hope this is the case, but when it comes to adult offspring who live with another without the benefit of marriage we say that it's a sign of the times, just the way things are. When older couples (even seniors) live together without being married because of financial advantage or simple convenience, few of us will dare to challenge their living situation as sinful.

St. John Chrysostom, a great preacher and teacher of the early Church, wrote, "Mortify your bodily members. These are things to avoid: fornication, uncleanness, passion, evil desire, and covetousness.

From these comes the wrath of God upon the sons of disobedience."

You and I are called to a decision about sin in our world. I haven't always done a good job with this challenge, and I suspect perhaps you have not always done a great job either. It's very hard in our culture to not only remain faithful to the Church's sexual ethics but also challenge our loved ones to do the same.

Somehow, in love, we need to share with our kids or those we can speak with about such things: sex belongs within the marriage. Only there. While our job is not to judge the person, we are called to share what we believe about the sanctity of marriage and the beautiful gift that physical love brings to husband and wife.

ACT

Today, I will take up the mantle of the Gospel in any way that the Lord Jesus and his Spirit lead me to do. I will speak or write in love. I will not flinch from truth.

PRAY

Lord God, we have given up the holy ground that you have gifted us with. Our ways of thinking and our practices have become weakened and defiled. "Restore us to You, O Lord, that we may be restored; Renew our days as of old" (Lamentations 5:21). Amen.

Tuesday, April 4
Fifth Week of Lent

BEGIN

Enter into silence and return to the Lord with your whole heart!

PRAY

With the Lord there is mercy
And fullness of redemption.

~Psalm 130:7

LISTEN

Read John 8:21–30

"Where I am going you cannot come."

~John 8:21b

Meet Me Where I Am

There is a Christian singer and musician named Noelle Garcia who recorded a song titled "Meet Me Where I Am." The words of the lyrics suggest that in our wanderings and travels, God meets us where we are. Another way of looking at this is, of course, that God is always waiting for us to find him no matter where we are.

In today's gospel reading, Jesus says to the Pharisees, "Where I am going, you cannot come" (John 8:21). The Pharisees ask one another if Jesus might be threatening suicide. But Jesus was speaking of his return to the Father. Like him, we look forward to our return to the Father, the one from whom all goodness comes. As we draw near the final days of Lent, Jesus the Good Shepherd is waiting to lead us to the pasture of eternal happiness. He guards us and cares for us and leads us ever onward toward more perfect union with the Father. Christ does this most especially through the sacraments of the Church. There he meets us precisely where we are.

ACT

Today, I will look at myself in a mirror and think about where I am in my walk with Jesus. Am I where I want to be? Is my heart open to his company and my soul committed to doing the Father's will? If I answer "no" to any of these questions, I will let go of whatever is holding me back.

PRAY

Lord Jesus, help me walk alongside you, healing, loving, serving. Be my companion and my guide. Amen.

WEDNESDAY, APRIL 5
FIFTH WEEK OF LENT

BEGIN

Enter into silence and return to the Lord with your whole heart!

PRAY

With the Lord there is mercy
And fullness of redemption.

~Psalm 130:7

LISTEN

Read John 8:31–42

Jesus answered them, "Amen, amen, I say to you, everyone who commits sin is a slave of sin."

~John 8:34

Truly Free

Lent is all about freedom. It is our annual time of spiritual renewal when we are urged by the Church to stop living as we usually do and to fast, to make additional time for prayer, and to be especially attentive to the poor in our midst by giving them what help we are able. We do these things not in a vacuum, but in order to set our priorities straight again, to free ourselves from whatever may have a hold on our time, energy, hearts, and minds that is *not* from God.

Far too many of us let sin be a somewhat abstract concept in our lives. We have a hard time being consistently mindful of ways in which we sin each day. We tend to relativize right and wrong, good and evil, preferring to remain quiet in the face of injustice, harmful relationships, greed, apathy, and the like. It is far easier to tell ourselves that what is right for me is not necessarily right for everyone. But the Christian life demands of us a higher standard.

As a deacon, I have been involved in marriage preparation ministry for a number of years. I believe it's safe to say that upwards of 75 percent of the couples I've worked with are already living together. It's a situation I try to address with them as we move into marriage preparation. Many live together for financial reasons, because they believe doing so will lead to a stronger marriage, or simply for convenience. Most seem not to have really thought about the deeper implications of the arrangement, and some seem to lack the facility to engage in conversation about right and wrong beyond an attitude of "no one is getting hurt so it's fine."

Discipleship demands more of us in considering how we live each day. It demands that we pray, celebrate the sacraments, and read and reflect on scripture so that we remain close to Christ. With him as our constant companion and guide, our sin will be more apparent to us, and our thirst for the freedom Christ alone can bring will grow strong.

ACT

> I will seek an opportunity to increase my spiritual practice. I will ask God for the gifts of discernment, and for freedom from any area of my life where I am enslaved to old wounds or to sin.

PRAY

> Remember no more the sins of my youth;
>   remember me according to your mercy, because
> of your goodness, LORD.

~Psalm 25:7

THURSDAY, APRIL 6
FIFTH WEEK OF LENT

BEGIN

Enter into silence and return to the Lord with your whole heart!

PRAY

With the Lord there is mercy
And fullness of redemption.

~Psalm 130:7

LISTEN

Read John 8:51–59

Jesus said to them, "Amen, amen, I say to you,
before Abraham came to be, I AM."
So they picked up stones to throw at him;
But Jesus hid and went out of the temple area.

~John 8:58

Suffering in the Christian Life

The expression I AM doesn't connote much to many of us; we are not biblical scholars. The message that God speaks to Moses in the story of Moses before the burning bush is paraphrased like this: "If I give you a name for me—I will be ordinary. I will be like each of you who has a name. You will not receive a human-sounding name for me. Because I AM eternal. I existed before you. I existed in a way that does not require a name."

This leads us to a relevant part of the dialogue Jesus has with the Jews in today's gospel reading. "Amen, amen, I say to you, before Abraham came to be, I AM" (John 8:58). Jesus uses language which must have been very understandable to both the leaders and the followers of Jewish faith. Jesus equates himself with God. He uses the same words as Yahweh did in Exodus. No wonder they reached for stones to throw at Jesus—he was claiming to be God.

On more than one occasion, Jesus found himself in grave danger. As a newborn, Herod's soldiers threatened him. A mob hostile to his preaching once tried to throw him off a cliff. And in today's gospel, he faces a stone-wielding crowd. But on all of these occasions, Jesus escaped from the violence. That's good for us to reflect on. Sometimes we think that as a follower of Jesus we need to accept and absorb whatever suffering may come our way. We recall Jesus' words that we should turn the other cheek when struck, and that all who follow him should expect to carry a cross, just like he did.

But following Jesus doesn't mean becoming a doormat or a punching bag. Suffering will indeed come our way. Some of it we're meant to embrace, so we might become more like Jesus. But some, as Jesus himself shows us, we will do best to avoid.

ACT

Today I will contemplate the meaning of suffering. Do I see it as a necessary part of being a follower of Jesus? Do I sometimes perceive it as punishment for sin? I will pray for deeper understanding and seek guidance from my pastor or other spiritual guide.

PRAY

Lord Jesus, you were crucified because you boldly preached the truth of God's saving power. May I find courage as I seek to do the will of the Father each and every day. Amen.

Friday, April 7
Fifth Week of Lent

BEGIN

Enter into silence and return to the Lord with your whole heart!

PRAY

With the Lord there is mercy
And fullness of redemption.

~Psalm 130:7

LISTEN

Read John 10:31–42

"If I do not perform my Father's works, do not believe me."

~John 10:37

Coming to Amen

Today's gospel ends with testimony to and about Jesus: "everything John said about this man was true." And so we have one form of arriving at truth explained for us. It's the acceptable testimony of someone who is trustworthy, to which we can say *Amen*.

Isn't there another, more potent form of arriving at truth? Jesus said so in Acts 1:8: "But you will receive power when the holy Spirit comes upon you, and you will be my witnesses in Jerusalem, throughout Judea and Samaria, and to the ends of the earth." Receiving the Holy Spirit creates an unstoppable witness to truth.

We receive the Holy Spirit at Baptism, and are strengthened by the Spirit's gifts in Confirmation. In 2008, Pope Benedict XVI said: "In effect, Jesus' whole mission was aimed at giving the Spirit of God to us and baptizing us in the 'bath' of regeneration." At a 2013 Pentecost audience, Pope Francis spoke of the Holy Spirit as an inexhaustible source of God's life in us. Both popes are suggesting regeneration of the way we live and witness to Christ in our lives. Ready yourself for the power of the Holy Spirit as you prepare to enter Holy Week.

ACT

Today I will read about the Seven Gifts of the Holy Spirit in *the Catechism of the Catholic Church*, at usccb. org or another online source. I will chose one thing I can do before Easter to witness to others the power of these gifts in my life.

PRAY

Come Holy Spirit, fill my heart with the fire of your love. Make of me a faithful witness to the tender mercy and mighty love of the Father. Amen.

Saturday, April 8
Fifth Week of Lent

BEGIN

Enter into silence and return to the Lord with your whole heart!

PRAY

With the Lord there is mercy
And fullness of redemption.

~Psalm 130:7

LISTEN

Read John 11:45–56

So the chief priests and the Pharisees convened the Sanhedrin and said, "What are we going to do?"

~John 11:47

Tension Mounts in Conflict

As we arrive at the late hours of our long Lent together, we see conflict and tension growing. As bestselling author Matthew Kelly puts it, Jesus was a radical. Make no mistake. The Son of Man was not here to accommodate the thinking of the sons of men.

Jesus wasn't controlled or manipulated by the political correctness that infects our modernity. He called people to follow him, barely hanging their wet fishing nets and leaving everything behind. Jesus spoke truth, and truth is radical. It causes tension and sometimes outright conflict.

That was the human drama unfolding two thousand years ago as those in positions of power are made uncomfortable and challenged by Jesus' words,

"I AM." Many of the same tensions between religious leaders are still found today. Every day we see in the news horrific violence perpetrated in the name of religion—not only between people of different faiths but also within the same religions: Muslims fighting Muslims, Christians lashing out to do physical or psychological and spiritual harm to other Christians. Jesus was no stranger to religious conflict, nor are we.

As faithful followers of the Lord Jesus, we are called to speak out against religious persecution in our own country and throughout the world. Pray for peace and take action on behalf of justice.

ACT

Today I will examine my own attitudes toward those of religious backgrounds different than my own and make a plan to find out more about one religious community with which I am unfamiliar.

PRAY

Heavenly Father, open my heart and mind to all people of faith. May I grow to understand those who are different than me and always be a faithful witness to Christ's redeeming love. Amen.

SUNDAY, APRIL 9
PALM SUNDAY OF THE LORD'S PASSION

BEGIN

Enter into silence and return to the Lord with your whole heart!

PRAY

But you, O Lord, be not far from me;
O my help, hasten to aid me.

~*Psalm 122:20*

LISTEN

Read Matthew 26:14–27:66

And kneeling before him, they mocked him, saying
"Hail King of the Jews!"

~*Matthew 27:29*

A Week of Contrasts and Challenge

The great liturgical passage into Holy Week opens before the lives of every practicing Christian. Who am I? Am I one waving palms as Jesus rides on a donkey? Am I an angel sent to console Jesus in the garden? Am I the one who denied him at the charcoal fire? Am I the one crying "Crucify him"? This week is a week to ask where you find yourself in the story. This week is a week to pray and then decide what kind of a follower of Christ you are going to be—for this Holy Week, and from now on.

This is a sweeping, busy week of liturgies and traditions. It is a week of stark contrast. While our gospel for today narrates the lengthy telling of Jesus' passion, liturgically we receive blessed palms. And yet, we should meditate upon one fact: pain without purpose is meaningless. Christ's suffering and death is rendered unbelievably beautiful because its origin is in love. And as we get a chance to journey closely with him, we can weep, repent, and love. In all of these, we can mitigate a part of the great suffering our sins have brought about in the Passion. And of course, we have the wonderful Easter Vigil Mass on Saturday evening.

Let none of us be Sunday-only Catholics this week. Let us be active participants in celebrating and living the great Paschal Mystery—that Christ died and rose again that we too will experience life everlasting.

ACT

Today I will clear my schedule of any usual tasks I can set aside. I will make plans to attend Holy Week liturgies with my fellow pilgrims in the faith. This Holy Week, I will be an active participant with Jesus, my Lord and my Savior.

PRAY

Lord Jesus, as I begin this most holy of weeks, be my constant companion. Help me enter fully into the mystery of your death and resurrection and steady my faith. Amen.

MONDAY, APRIL 10
HOLY WEEK

BEGIN

Enter into silence and return to the Lord with your whole heart!

PRAY

But you, O Lord, be not far from me;
O my help, hasten to aid me.

~Psalm 22:20

LISTEN

Read John 12:1–11

Mary took a liter of costly perfumed oil . . . and anointed the feet of Jesus and dried them with her hair.

~John 12:3

The Aroma of Love

As we suggested in the Passion Sunday reflection, this is a week of emotional swings. In our liturgical readings there is the tension: the hatred, the plotting of the leaders seeking to end the "troubles" caused by this unconventional, challenging teacher, Jesus, whose influence continues to swell. There are whispers: "Do you think he will come to the (Passover) feast? Maybe we can do something about all this then."

And six days before the actual Passover, Jesus slips away to Bethany for quiet time with those he loved. Little did those closest to Jesus really know what was to happen in just a few days. No. Here, there is the aroma of Martha's marvelous cooking. The scent of expensive oil on Jesus. So many beautiful aspects as we try to realize what is happening in our Holy Week thoughts.

Who reclines across from Jesus, with direct eye-to-eye contact? The one he had raised from the dead. In fact, the gaze shared from time to time between the two of them suggests the powerful and intimate relationship they share. Those attending the dinner (and we who are seeking to capture every detail of this scene) may not understand what it is, but we recognize there is some special knowledge that Lazarus was gifted with.

These moments can yield so much for us as we enter into the story and meaning of the final days and hours in the life of our Savior.

ACT

Today, I will recall and meditate on what it means to be called to serve the Lord and his Church in two ways: In my service to my fellow people, and in my service to the visible beauty of the Church in all of its liturgies. I will commit to supporting both.

PRAY

Lord God, be my strength this day. Lead me deeper into the mystery of your abiding love and tender mercy. Amen.

TUESDAY, APRIL 11
HOLY WEEK

BEGIN

Enter into silence and return to the Lord with your whole heart!

PRAY

But you, O Lord, be not far from me;
O my help, hasten to aid me.

~Psalm 22:20

LISTEN

Read John 13:21–33; 36–38

After Judas took the morsel, Satan entered him.

~John 13:27

Two Kinds of Betrayal

There is a man of good heart: he's a volunteer who does much for his parish and in the local community. But he has a characteristic like Peter: he speaks before most anything is weighed, measured, or thought out in advance. The result? Things are said that aren't correct and strident opinions given which should have been tempered. Have you met someone like this? Peter was like this: periodically brash and opinionated, but always loving the Master.

Today's gospel presents two betrayals that are soon to happen: the horrible disloyalty of Judas and Peter's charcoal fire lies: "Woman, I do not know him" (Luke 22:57).

What is the difference between the two betrayals? Are not both guilty of the same sin, and to the same degree? Perhaps not. Scripture suggests that the accountant Judas sinfully handled money for the group. And he had time to meet with authorities to plan and commit to his evil. Whereas Peter momentarily loses it when, in surprise, he is confronted by accusers. His betrayal is perhaps simply a momentary loss of courage.

Throughout scripture, God has used the weak, the confused, the brash, and sinners. But they were men and women ready to repent and change their ways. I don't know if we ought to celebrate our weaknesses, but we can take them to the foot of the Cross and admit them to the Lord. Repentance and renewal is on the way. The stone in front of your tomb can also be rolled back.

ACT

If able to participate in the Good Friday Celebration of the Lord's Passion, I will go forward to reverence the cross, bringing my list of weaknesses. I will kiss the cross and ask for his grace to work within me for a conversion of life.

PRAY

Oh my God, I am heartily sorry for having offended thee. I detest all my sins because of your just punishments, but most of all because they have offended you my God, who are all good and worthy of all my love. I firmly resolve with the help of your grace to sin no more and to avoid the near occasions of sin. Amen.

~Act of Contrition

WEDNESDAY, APRIL 12
HOLY WEEK

BEGIN

Enter into silence and return to the Lord with your whole heart!

PRAY

But you, O Lord, be not far from me;
O my help, hasten to aid me.

~Psalm 22:20

LISTEN

Read Matthew 26:14–25

On the first day of the Feast of Unleavened Bread, the disciples approached Jesus and said, "Where do you want us to prepare for you to eat the Passover?"

~Matthew 26:17

The Meal Honoring the Exodus

"Hurry. Get out while you can." Perhaps 1,450 years before the time of Christ, these were the words of the God of the Jewish people on the evening after the Passover. "Don't spend time gathering yeast. Just bake your bread without leaven and then leave." They were to exit quickly from their slavery in the land of Egypt.

And for hundreds of years following, Passover was one day and night. But the Feast of Unleavened Bread lasted seven days. Our gospel for today tells of the first of the seven days, a day to get ready for the Passover meal. The practice of Lent, and now this beautiful and powerful holiest of weeks, gives us a chance to repeat our two-thousand-year-old faith traditions over and over. And so, there was Passion Sunday and the blessed palms. Beginning at sundown tomorrow we celebrate the great Easter Triduum with the Mass of the Lord's Supper when we will commemorate the Last Supper and the institution of the Eucharist. In many places priests renew their priestly commitment early on Holy Thursday at the Chrism Mass when the sacred oils used in the sacraments are blessed.

Good Friday follows as we recall and accept as our own the Passion and Death of Jesus. Then Holy Saturday as we wait and fast until the great Easter Vigil when we celebrate the Resurrection. Then on into Sunday with praise and worship during several Masses in most parishes. Finally at sundown on Easter Sunday the last liturgical celebration of the Triduum is held in many places—First Vespers of Easter.

These most sacred liturgies help us recall the week that Jesus and his followers experienced: from the joy of Jesus' being carried by a donkey at his entry into the city, to his being carried to a tomb only to be raised again by the Father.

ACT

I will enter into all of the beauty and tragedy and drama of this week, beginning today with reflection on what sinfulness keeps me from union with Christ. I will journey with Jesus to the Cross, the tomb, and in the end to the glory of the Resurrection.

PRAY

Blessed are you, Our God, Ruler of the world. In the Church founded by your Son, we pray and celebrate the festivals of your chosen people. Sanctify these hours and hear our prayers. Amen.

The Easter Triduum
April 13
Holy Thursday

BEGIN

Enter into silence and return to the Lord.

PRAY

The cup of salvation I will take up,
and I will call upon the name of the Lord.

~*Psalm 116:13*

LISTEN

Read John 13:1–15

And he began to wash the disciples' feet and dry
them with the towel around his waist.

~*John 13:8*

The First Mass

Imagine being at the last supper as a disciple of Jesus.

Tonight he seems unusually loving. He shared
a look of deepest caring as he greeted each of us. He
leads us in prayer. We eat and we share memories and
joys of things seen and done. Then he stops talking.
One by one we become quiet, looking at him, waiting.

"This is my body that is for you. Do this in
remembrance of me." And then, after giving us pieces
of bread, he repeats the action with that beautiful cup.
We've eaten a hundred suppers with him, yet somehow, this is different. We don't really understand. But
something has entered us and we are changed.

April 14
Good Friday

BEGIN

Enter into silence and return to the Lord.

PRAY

The cup of salvation I will take up,
and I will call upon the name of the Lord.

~Psalm 116:13

LISTEN

Read John 18:1–19:42

Jesus answered, "I told you that I AM."

~John 18:8

Whom Are You Looking For?

"Whom are you looking for?" They sought Jesus. His reply booms throughout Old and New Testaments: "I AM." Two words said and they turned away and fell to the ground. When humans seek the God of Abraham, the experience of his grace and truth is powerful. For believers, it is beautiful.

In St. Augustine's *Confessions*, we read how Augustine heard a loud cry that shattered his deafness; Augustine saw radiant beauty and smelled fragrance unlike anything ever before.

In the liturgy today, we weep and bury our Savior. We recall our sins and wounded souls. These, too, we meet with weeping, then bury them with Christ.

We silently await Resurrection.

April 15

Holy Saturday

Enter into silence and return to the Lord.

PRAY

The cup of salvation I will take up,
and I will call upon the name of the Lord.

~Psalm 116:13

LISTEN

Read Matthew 28:1–10

Then they went away quickly from the tomb,
fearful yet overjoyed, and ran to announce this to
his disciples.

~Matthew 28:8

How Can This Be?

The words of the two Marys: How can it be? We
wrapped him in burial cloth and placed him in his
tomb. We don't understand; the tomb is now empty.
Quick, let's run! Run to tell Peter and the others. I don't
think they'll believe us. I want to cry. I want to fall on
my knees and pray.

But that beautiful, light-surrounded man said to
"go quickly and tell the disciples." Not only them, I'll
tell everyone we see along the way. "Jesus was dead.
But he has risen! He is alive. And so am I."

April 16

Easter Sunday

Exult, let them exult, the hosts of heaven,
exult, let Angel ministers of God exult,
let the trumpet of salvation
sound aloud our mighty King's triumph!
Be glad, let earth be glad, as glory floods her,
ablaze with light from her eternal King,
let all corners of the earth be glad,
knowing an end to gloom and darkness.
Rejoice, let Mother Church also rejoice,
arrayed with the lightning of his glory,
let this holy building shake with joy,
filled with the mighty voices of the peoples.
It is truly right and just, with ardent love of mind and heart
and with devoted service of our voice,
to acclaim our God invisible, the almighty Father,
and Jesus Christ, our Lord, his Son, his Only Begotten.
Who for our sake paid Adam's debt to the eternal Father,
and, pouring out his own dear Blood,
wiped clean the record of our ancient sinfulness.

~From the Exsultet or Easter Proclamation

Deacon Tom Fox was ordained by Archbishop Charles Chaput in 2004 in Denver. He served the Archdiocese of Denver from 2004 to 2007 in parish ministry in Estes Park, Colorado. In late 2007, Fox and his wife, Dee, moved to Arizona where he serves the Tucson Diocese in Payson. In 2013, he was named associate deacon of Madonna House, a predominantly lay community that operates a number of field houses of hospitality and formation.

Fox writes columns and records audio reflections for websites such as *CatholicMom.com* and *Catholic Moments*. He also has been a periodic columnist for *Catholic Family*. In 2009, the Foxes started the *Catholic Vitamins* website and podcast. In 2015, he and three colleagues began KPIH 98.9 Rim Catholic Radio—an affiliate of the Immaculate Heart Radio Network—in their north central Arizona community. Fox is president of the Rim Catholic Evangelization Association and an active member of the Catholic Radio Association.